Five Hundred *and* One
Kosher Quotes

Five Hundred *and* One
Kosher Quotes

DORON KORNBLUTH

ISBN: 978-1-952370-28-1

Published by Jonah Press
A division of Mosaica Press, Inc.

Printed in Bulgaria

TABLE OF CONTENTS

ADVERSITY

1 Nearly all men can stand adversity, but if you want to test a man's character, give him power.

Abraham Lincoln

2 He knows not his own strength that hath not met adversity.

Ben Jonson

3 You will never truly know yourself or the strength of your relationships until both have been tested by adversity.

J. K. Rowling

4

In prosperity our friends know us; in adversity we know our friends.

John Churton Collins

5

Adversity does teach who your real friends are.

Lois McMaster Bujold

6

Remember that there is nothing stable in human affairs; therefore avoid undue elation in prosperity, or undue depression in adversity.

Socrates

7 Adversity causes some men to break; others to break records.

William Arthur Ward

8 Although the world is full of suffering, it is also full of the overcoming of it.

Helen Keller

9

Mishaps are like knives that either serve us or cut us, as we grasp them by the blade or the handle.

James Russell Lowell

10

The greatest *university* is *adversity*.

Shraga Silverstein

11

Man needs difficulties; they are necessary for health.

Carl Jung

12

You'll never find a better sparring partner than adversity.

Walt Schmidt

AMERICA

13

America is the only nation in history which miraculously has gone directly from barbarism to denigration without the usual interval of civilization.

George Clemenceau

14

In America, any boy may become President—and I suppose it's just one of the risks he takes.

Adlai E. Stevenson Jr.

15

America's one of the finest countries anyone ever stole.

Bobcat Goldthwaite

16

There's the country of America, which you have to defend, but there's also the idea of America. America is more than just a country, it's an idea. An idea that's supposed to be contagious.

Bono

17

There is nothing wrong with America that the faith, love of freedom, intelligence, and energy of her citizens cannot cure.

Dwight D. Eisenhower

18

The United States is a nation of laws: badly written and randomly enforced.

Frank Zappa

19

A citizen of America will cross the ocean to fight for democracy, but won't cross the street to vote in a national election.

Bill Vaughan

20

My fellow Americans, ask not what your country can do for you—ask what you can do for your country.

John F. Kennedy

21 *The almighty dollar, that great object of universal devotion throughout our land.*

Washington Irving

22 The thing that impresses me most about America is the way parents obey their children.

Edward, Duke of Windsor

23 America is so vast that almost everything said is likely to be true, and the opposite is probably equally true.

James T. Farrel

24

There's is nothing that is wrong with America that can't be fixed with what is right with America.

Bill Clinton

25 America a land of wonders, in which everything is in constant motion and every change seems an improvement...No natural boundary seems to be set to the efforts of man; and in his eyes what is not yet done is only what he has not yet attempted to do.

Alexis De Tocqueville

26

America is a large friendly dog in a very small room. Every time it wags its tail, it knocks over a chair.

A. J. Toynbee

27

The youth of America is their oldest tradition. It has been going on now for three hundred years.

Oscar Wilde

28 *The business of America is business.*

Calvin Coolidge

29

The business of America is not business. Neither is it war. The business of America is justice and securing the blessings of liberty.

George F. Will

30

Too many of us look upon Americans as dollar chasers. This is a cruel libel, even if it is reiterated thoughtlessly by the Americans themselves.

Albert Einstein

31

Americans will put up with anything provided it doesn't block traffic.

Dan Rather

32

I was born an American; I will live an American; I shall die an American.

Daniel Webster

33 Americans never quit.

General Douglas Macarthur

34

Americans are over-reachers; overreaching is the most admirable of the many American excesses.

George F. Will

35 Half of the American people have never read a newspaper. Half never voted for President. One hopes it is the same half.

Gore Vidal

36

Nobody ever went broke underestimating the intelligence of the American public.

H. L. Mencken

37

George Washington had a vision for this country. Was it three days of uninterrupted shopping?

Jeff Melvoin

38

The American, by nature, is optimistic. He is experimental, an inventor and a builder who builds best when called upon to build greatly.

John F. Kennedy

39

America has never been an empire. We may be the
only great power in history that had the chance,
and refused—preferring greatness to power and
justice to glory.

George W. Bush

40

In a country as big as the United
States, you can find fifty examples
of anything.

Jeffery F. Chamberlain

41

In Boston they ask, 'How much does
he know?' In New York, 'How much is
he worth?' In Philadelphia, 'Who were
his parents?'

Mark Twain

42

You know that being an American is more than a
matter of where your parents came from. It is a belief

that all men are created free and equal and that
everyone deserves an even break.

Harry S. Truman

43

For other nations, utopia is a blessed past
never to be recovered; for Americans it is
just beyond the horizon.

Henry Kissinger

44

It's a glorious time to be an American but the glories
come at you so relentlessly, so multitudinously, that
they will finish you off unless you ration the intake.
Nikita Kruschev, poor dolt, once said the Soviet Union
would bury us. He didn't know that left alone, we
would bury ourselves under our own riches.

Russel Baker

ANGER

45

Anger makes you smaller, while
forgiveness forces you to grow beyond
what you were.

Cherie Carter-Scott

46

If you do not wish to be prone to anger, do not feed the
habit; give it nothing which may tend to its increase.

Epictetus

47

I have seen a peaceful expression
turn to anger as fast as a whip
cracks, and so the look on the face
might mean less than what
it seems to be.

Erica Eisdorfer

48

Holding on to anger, resentment, and hurt only gives you tense muscles, a headache, and a sore jaw from clenching your teeth. Forgiveness gives you back the laughter and the lightness in your life.

Joan Lunden

49

Speak when you are angry—and you will make the best speech you'll ever regret.

Laurence J. Peter

50

How much more grievous are the consequences
of anger than the causes of it.

Marcus Aurelius

51

Never get angry. Never make a threat.
Reason with people.

Mario Puzo

ANTI-SEMITISM

52

The Jews are a frightened people.
Nineteen centuries of Christian love have
broken their nerves.

Israel Zangwill

53

The world is divided into two groups of nations—
those which want to expel the Jews and those which
do not want to receive them.

Chaim Weizmann

54

To the injustice committed in our
name we must not add the injustice
of forgetting.

Hannah Vogt

55

I know of no crime in the history of mankind more horrible in its details than the treatment of the Jews.

Major Walsh at Nuremberg Trials

56 *Wherever they burn books, they will also, in the end, burn human beings.*

Heinrich Heine

57

Some accuse me of being a Jew, others forgive me for being a Jew, still others praise me for it. But all of them reflect upon it.

Laqueur—Borne

ART

58

One reassuring thing about modern art is that things can't be as bad as they are painted.

M. Walthall Jackson

59

Without tradition, art is a flock of sheep without a shepherd. Without innovation, it is a corpse.

Sir Winston Churchill

60

Art is a lie that makes us realize the truth.

Pablo Picasso

61

[Abstract art is] a product of the untalented, sold by the unprincipled to the utterly bewildered.

Al Capp

62 *Painting: The art of protecting flat surfaces from the weather and exposing them to the critic.*

Ambrose Bierce

63

I have often thought that if photography were difficult in the true sense of the term—meaning that the creation of a simple photograph would entail as much time and effort as the production of a good watercolor or etching—there would be a vast improvement in total output. The sheer ease with which we can produce a superficial image often leads to creative disaster.

Ansel Adams

64

I suppose no matter what I'm drawing, there will always be some sort of question in my mind about it. A work of art (even cartoon art) is never really finished; it is abandoned.

Brooke McEldowney

65

I can't criticize what I don't understand. If you want to call this art, you've got the benefit of all my doubts.

Charles Rosin

66

Art forms of the past were really considered elitist. Bach did not compose for the masses, neither did Beethoven. It was always for patrons, aristocrats, and royalty. Now we have a sort of democratic version of that, which is to say that the audience is so splintered in its interests.

David Cronenberg

67

If you were in a burning house and there was a cat and a Rembrandt, what would you save? The cat...you would save the cat, because the cat is alive. The art is dead. It's just paint on a canvas, ink on a page. To live for art is to deny life. It's just to destroy life.

Diane Frolov and Andrew Schneider

Another unsettling element in modern art is that common symptom of immaturity, the dread of doing what has been done before.

Edith Wharton

69

A painting in a museum hears more ridiculous opinions than anything else in the world.

Edmond de Goncourt

70

It is all very well, when the pen flows, but then there are the dark days when imagination deserts one, and it is an effort to put anything down on paper. That little you have achieved stares at you at the end of the day, and you know the next morning you will have to scrape it down and start again.

Elizabeth Aston

71

I don't believe in total freedom for the artist. Left on his own, free to do anything he likes, the artist ends up doing nothing at all. If there's one thing that's dangerous for an artist, it's precisely this question of total freedom, waiting for inspiration and all the rest of it.

Federico Fellini

72

Art is making something out of nothing and selling it.

Frank Zappa

73

Art, like morality, consists of drawing the line somewhere.

G. K. Chesterton

BOOKS

74

Reading, after a certain age, diverts the mind too much from its creative pursuits. Any man who reads too much and uses his own brain too little falls into lazy habits of thinking.

Albert Einstein

75

This paperback is very interesting, but I find it will never replace a hardcover book—it makes a very poor doorstop.

Alfred Hitchcock

76

The covers of this book are too far apart.

Ambrose Bierce

77

A room without books is as a body without a soul.

Lord Avebury

78

There's a certain kind of conversation you have from time to time at parties in New York about a new book. The word "banal" sometimes rears its by-now banal head; you say "under-edited," I say "derivative." The conversation goes around and around various literary criticisms, and by the time it moves on one thing is clear: No one read the book; we just read the reviews.

Anna Quindlen

79

The number of books will grow continually, and one can predict that a time will come when it will be almost as difficult to learn anything from books as from the direct study of the whole universe. It will be almost as convenient to search for some bit of truth concealed in nature as it will be to find it hidden away in an immense multitude of bound volumes.

Denis Diderot

80

Books to the ceiling,
Books to the sky,
My pile of books is a mile high.
How I love them! How I need them!
I'll have a long beard by the time I
read them.

Arnold Lobel

81

Wear the old coat and buy
the new book.

Austin Phelps

82

Life-transforming ideas have always come to me through books.

Bell Hooks

83

Many books require no thought from those who read them, and for a very simple reason; they made no such demand upon those who wrote them.

Charles Caleb Colton

84

This is not a novel to be tossed aside lightly. It should be thrown with great force.

Dorothy Parker

85

Most new books are forgotten within a year, especially by those who borrow them.

Evan Esar

86

A good novel tells us the truth about its hero; but a bad novel tells us the truth about its author.

G. K. Chesterton

87

From the moment I picked up your book until I laid it down, I was convulsed with laughter. Someday I intend reading it.

Groucho Marx

COMMUNICATION

88 Real communication happens when people feel safe.

Ken Blanchard

89 The real art of conversation is not only to say the right thing at the right place but to leave unsaid the wrong thing at the tempting moment.

Dorothy Nevill

90

Few are agreeable in conversation, because each thinks more of what he intends to say than of what others are saying, and listens no more when he himself has a chance to speak.

Francois de La Rochefoucauld

91 *Anecdotes and maxims are rich treasures to the man of the world, for he knows how to introduce the former at fit place in conversation.*

Johann Wolfgang von Goethe

92

One of the best rules in conversation is never to say a thing which any of the company can reasonably wish had been left unsaid.

Jonathan Swift

93

Most conversations are simply monologues delivered in the presence of witnesses.

Margaret Millar

94

The character of a man is known from his conversations.

Menander

95

Conversation is food for the soul.

Mexican Proverb

96

You can discover more about a person in an hour of play than in a year of conversation.

Plato

97

Don't knock the weather. If it didn't change once in a while, nine out of ten people couldn't start a conversation.

Kin Hubbard

98

When you have nothing to say, say nothing.

Charles Caleb Colton

99

Small minds discuss people, average minds discuss events, great minds discuss ideas.

Anonymous

100

Let us make a special effort to stop communicating with each other, so we can have some conversation.

Judith Martin

101

Think like a wise man but communicate in the language of the people.

William Butler Yeats

102

Good communication is as stimulating as black coffee and just as hard to sleep after.

Anne Morrow Lindbergh

103

No one has a finer command of language that the person who keeps his mouth shut.

Sam Rayburn

104

Don't *say* things. What you *are* stands over you the while, and thunders so that I cannot hear what you say to the contrary.

Ralph Waldo Emerson

105

As I get older, I've learned to listen to people rather than accuse them of things.

Po Bronson

106

Don't confuse being "soft" with seeing the other guy's point of view.

George Bush

107

Listening is as important as talking. If you're a good listener, people often compliment you for being a good conversationalist.

Gov. Jesse Ventura

108

Seek first to understand and then to be understood. Most people do not listen with the intent to understand: they listen with the intent to reply. They're filtering everything through their own paradigms, reading their autobiography into other people's lives.

Stephen R. Covey

DEMOCRACY
AND FREEDOM

109

Democracy is only an experiment in government, and it has the obvious disadvantage of merely counting votes instead of weighing them.

W. R. Inge

110

Democracy is the recurrent suspicion that more than half of the people are right more than half of the time.

E.B. White

111

*I think we must
agree that
the fools are
in a terrible
overwhelming
majority, all the
wide world over.*

Henrik Ibsen

112

Many forms of Government have been tried, and
will be tried in this world of sin and woe. No one
pretends that democracy is perfect or all-wise. Indeed,
it has been said that democracy is the worst form of
government except all those other forms that have
been tried from time to time.

Sir Winston Churchill

113

Democracy consists of choosing your dictators after they've told you what you think it is you want to hear.

Alan Corenk

114

Democracy means government by the uneducated, while aristocracy means government by the badly educated.

G. K. Chesterton

115

Democracy is a device that ensures we shall be governed no better than we deserve.

George Bernard Shaw

116

Democracy is a process by which the people are free to choose the man who will get the blame.

Laurence J. Peter

117

Under democracy one party always devotes its chief energies to trying to prove that the other party is unfit to rule—and both commonly succeed, and are right.

H. L. Mencken

118

Democracy is based upon the conviction that there are extraordinary possibilities in ordinary people.

Harry Emerson Fosdick

119

The great thing about democracy is that it gives every voter a chance to do something stupid.

Art Spander

120

When great changes occur in history, when great principles are involved, as a rule the majority are wrong.

Eugene Debs

121

I do not believe in the collective wisdom of individual ignorance.

Thomas Carlyle

122

O liberty! O liberty! What crimes are committed in thy name!

Madame Jeanne-Marie Roland

123

Man is born free, and everywhere he is in chains.

Jean-Jacques Rousseau

124

Many politicians lay it down as a self-evident proposition that no people ought to be free until they are fit to use their freedom. The maxim is worthy of the fool in the old story who resolved not to go into the water until he had learned to swim.

Lord Macaulay

125

Our youth want freedom to be slaves of their impulses.

Shraga Silverstein

126

The most stringent protection of free speech would not protest a man falsely shouting fire in a theater and causing a panic.

Oliver Wendell Holmes, Jr.

127

Posterity: you will never know how much it has cost my generation to preserve your freedom. I hope you will make good use of it.

John Quincy Adams

128

I do not agree with what you have to say, but I'll defend to the death your right to say it.

Patrick Henry

EDUCATION

129

A teacher affects eternity.

Henry B. Adams

130

Educate men without religion and you make them but clever devils.

Duke of Wellington

131

Education does not mean teaching people to know what they do not know; it means teaching them to behave as they do not behave.

John Ruskin

132

I have never let my schooling interfere with my education.

Mark Twain

133

Treat a man as he is, and he will remain as he is. Treat a man as he could be, and he will become what he should be.

Ralph Waldo Emerson

134

Only the educated are free.

Epictetus

135

America believes in education: the average professor earns more money in a year than a professional athlete earns in a whole week.

Evan Esar

136

Education is simply the soul of a society as it passes from one generation to another.

G. K. Chesterton

137

College isn't the place to go for ideas.

Helen Keller

138

Bachelor's degrees make pretty good placemats if you get 'em laminated.

Jeph Jacques

139

Life at a university with its intellectual and inconclusive discussions at the postgraduate level is on the whole a bad training for the real world. Only men of very strong character surmount this handicap.

Sir Paul Chambers

140

Ye can lead a man up to the university but ye can't make him think.

Finley Peter Dunne

141

Education...has produced a vast population able to read but unable to distinguish what is worth reading.

G.M. Trevelyan

142

True education makes for inequality; the inequality of individuality, the inequality of success, the glorious inequality of talent, of genius.

Felix E. Scheling

143

Genius without education is like silver in the mine.

Benjamin Franklin

144

It is possible to store the mind with a million facts and still be entirely uneducated.

Alec Bourne

145

It is the mark of an educated mind to be able to entertain a thought without accepting it.

Aristotle

146

Education is what survives when what has been learned has been forgotten.

B. F. Skinner

147

Everyone has a right to a university degree in America, even if it's in Hamburger Technology.

Clive James

FEAR AND COURAGE

148

Be sure you put your feet in the right place, then stand firm

Abraham Lincoln

149

Courage is almost a contradiction in terms. It means a strong desire to live taking the form of a readiness to die.

G.K. Chesterton

150

A hero is no braver than an ordinary man, but he is brave five minutes longer.

R. W. Emerson

151

Courage is the ladder on which all the other virtues mount.

Clare Booth Luce

152

Courage is fear that has said its prayers.

Dorothy Bernard

153

Courage is doing what you're afraid to do. There can be no courage unless you're scared.

Eddie Rickenbacker

154

Perfect courage means doing unwitnessed what he would be capable of with the world looking on.

Francois de La Rochefoucauld

155

Courage is the art of being the only one who knows you're scared to death.

Harold Wilson

156

Courage is being scared to death—but saddling up anyway.

John Wayne

157

The worst thing of all is standing by when folks are doing something wrong.

Kirby Larson

158

It is curious that physical courage should be so common in the world and moral courage so rare.

Mark Twain

159

Keep your fears to yourself, but share your courage with others.

Robert Louis Stevenson

160

Courage is not the absence of fear but the ability to carry on with dignity in spite of it.

Scott Torow

161

Courage is resistance to fear, mastery of fear, not absence of fear.

Mark Twain

162

We experience moments absolutely free from worry. These brief respites are called panic.

Cullen Hightower

163

The only thing we have to fear is fear itself.

Franklin D. Roosevelt

FRIENDSHIP AND RELATIONSHIPS

164

Lots of people want to ride with you in the limo, but what you want is someone who will take the bus with you when the limo breaks down.

Oprah Winfrey

165

Friendship is like a bank account. You can't continue to draw on it without making deposits.

Bits & Pieces

166

There is no man so friendless but what he can find a friend sincere enough to tell him disagreeable truths.

Edward Bulwer-Lytton

167

Without friends no one would choose to live, though he had all other goods.

Aristotle

168

Being friendless taught me how to be a friend. Funny how that works.

Colleen Wainwright

169

Do not protect yourself by a fence, but rather by your friends.

Czech Proverb

170

You can make more friends in two months by becoming interested in other people than you can in two years by trying to get other people interested in you.

Dale Carnegie

171

Never explain— your friends do not need it and your enemies will not believe you anyway.

Elbert Hubbard

172

Nothing changes your opinion of a friend so surely
as success—yours or his.

Franklin P. Jones

173

All people want is someone
to listen.

Hugh Elliott

174

Go through your phone book, call people and ask them
to drive you to the airport. The ones who will drive
you are your true friends. The rest aren't bad people;
they're just acquaintances.

Jay Leno

175

When you build bridges you can keep
crossing them.

Rick Pitino

176

In prosperity our friends know us; in adversity we know our friends.

Churton Collins

177

An injury is much sooner forgotten than an insult.

Lord Chesterfield

178

A true friend is the greatest of all blessings, and the one that we take the least care of all to acquire.

La Rochefoucauld

179

The holy passion of friendship is of so sweet and steady and loyal and enduring a nature that it will last through a whole lifetime, if not asked to lend money.

Mark Twain

180

The only way to have friends is to be one.

Ralph Waldo Emerson

GOALS

181

You must have long range goals to keep you from being frustrated by short range failures.

Charles C. Noble

182

A goal without a plan is just a wish.

Antoine de Saint-Exupery

183

It is a paradoxical but profoundly true and important principle of life that the most likely way to reach a goal is to be aiming not at that goal itself but at some more ambitious goal beyond it.

Arnold Toynbee

184

The reason most people never reach their goals is that they don't define them, or ever seriously consider them as believable or achievable. Winners can tell you where they are going, what they plan to do along the way, and who will be sharing the adventure with them.

Denis Watley

185

Achievable goals are the first step to self-improvement.

J. K. Rowling

186

A successful individual typically sets his next goal somewhat but not too much above his last achievement. In this way he steadily raises his level of aspiration.

Kurt Lewin

187

We find no real satisfaction or happiness in life without obstacles to conquer and goals to achieve.

Maxwell Maltz

188

The big secret in life is that there is no big secret. Whatever your goal, you can get there if you're willing to work.

Oprah Winfrey

189

Do not turn back when you are just at the goal.

Publilius Syrus

190

In the absence of clearly defined goals, we become strangely loyal to performing daily trivia until ultimately we become enslaved by it.

Robert Heinlein

191

Slight not what's near through aiming at what's far.

Euripides

192

One does not discover new lands without consenting to lose sight of the shore for a very long time.

Andre Gide

GREATNESS

193

If a man has greatness in him,
it comes to light—not in one
flamboyant hour, but in the ledger
of his daily work.

Beryl Markham

194

Some men are born great,
some achieve greatness, and
some have greatness thrust
upon them.

William Shakespeare

195

Some are born great, some achieve greatness, and some
hire public relations officers.

Daniel J. Boorstin

196

Greatness is more than potential. It is the execution of that potential. Beyond the raw talent. You need the appropriate training. You need the discipline. You need the inspiration. You need the drive.

Eric A. Burns

197

We have, I fear, confused power with greatness.

Stewart L. Udall

198

The measure of a country's greatness is its ability to retain compassion in times of crisis.

Thurgood Marshall

199

Mediocrity knows nothing higher than itself, but talent instantly recognizes genius.

Sir Arthur Conan Doyle

200

Most of us will never do great things, but we can do small things in a great way.

Bits and Pieces

201

The price of greatness is responsibility.

Winston Churchill

202

Genius is nothing but a great aptitude for patience.

Georges Louis Leclerc

203

If you have integrity, nothing
else matters. If you don't have
integrity, nothing else matters.

Alan Simpson

204

In the end, integrity is all you've got.

Jack Welch

205

Excellence and competitiveness are totally compatible
with honesty and integrity. The A student, the four-
minute miler, the high jump record holder—all strong
winners—can achieve those results without resorting
to cheating. People who cheat are simply weak.

Jack Welch

206

We need heroes, people who can inspire us, help shape
us morally, spur us on to purposeful action—and
from time to time we are called on to be those heroes,

leaders for others, either in a small, day-to-day way, or on the world's larger stage.

Robert Coles

207

There are no speed limits on the road to excellence.

David W Johnson

208

I do the very best I know how…and I mean to do so until the end.

Abraham Lincoln

209

The glory of great men should always be measured by
the means they have used to acquire it.

La Rochefoucauld

210

Some people are more talented than
others. Some are more educationally
privileged than others. But we
all have the capacity to be great.
Greatness comes with recognizing
that your potential is limited only by
how you choose, how you use your
freedom, how resolute you are—
in short, by your attitude. And we are
all free to choose our attitude.

Peter Koestenbaum

211

We are what we repeatedly do.
Excellence then is not an act
but a habit.

Aristotle

212

Freedom to be your best means nothing unless you're willing to do your best.

Colin Powell

213

I would much rather have men ask why I have no statue than why I have one.

Cato the Elder

214

Great spirits have always found violent opposition from mediocrities. The latter cannot understand it when a man does not thoughtlessly submit to hereditary prejudices but honestly and courageously uses his intelligence.

Albert Einstein

215

The reward of a thing well done is having done it.

Ralph Waldo Emerson

216

To be great is to be misunderstood.

Ralph Waldo Emerson

217

Great work is done by people who are not afraid to be great.

Fernando Flores

218

Excellence is in the details. Give attention to the details and excellence will come.

Perry Paxton

219

Never doubt that a small group of thoughtful committed citizens can change the world, indeed it is the only thing that ever has.

Margaret Mead

HABIT

220

To fall into a habit is to begin to cease to be.

Miguel De Unamuno

221

The chains of habit are too weak to be felt until they are too strong to be broken.

Dr. Samuel Johnson

222

Motivation is what gets you started. Habit is what keeps you going.

Jim Ryun

223 *Curious things, habits. People themselves never knew they had them.*

Agatha Christie

224 My problem lies in reconciling my gross habits with my net income.

Errol Flynn

225

Habit is habit and not to be flung out of the window by any man, but coaxed downstairs a step at a time.

Mark Twain

226

Nothing is stronger than habit.

Ovid

227

Freedom is the right to choose the habits which bind you.

Renate Rubinstein

HAPPINESS

228

We have no more right to consume happiness without producing it than to consume wealth without producing it.

George Bernard Shaw

229

Short is the joy that guilty pleasure brings.

Euripides

230

I feel like a tiny bird with a big song!

Jerry Van Amerongen

231

I've grown to realize the joy that comes from little victories is preferable to the fun that comes from ease and the pursuit of pleasure.

Lawana Blackwell

232

Learning to live in the present moment is part of the path of joy.

Sarah Ban Breathnach

233

Real joy comes not from ease or riches or from the praise of men, but from doing something worthwhile.

Sir Wilfred Grenfell

234

Success is getting what you want. Happiness is wanting what you get.

Dale Carnegie

235

Happiness lies not in the mere possession of money. It lies in the joy of achievement, in the thrill of creative effort.

Franklin D. Roosevelt

236

Most folks are about as happy as they make up their minds to be.

Abraham Lincoln

237

Content makes poor men rich; discontentment makes rich men poor.

Benjamin Franklin

238

If there were in the world today any large number of people who desired their own happiness more than they desired the unhappiness of others, we could have paradise in a few years.

Bertrand Russell

239

The pursuit of happiness is a most ridiculous phrase; if you pursue happiness you'll never find it.

C. P. Snow

240

Cherish all your happy moments: they make a fine cushion for old age.

Christopher Morley

241

Slow down and enjoy life. It's not only the scenery you miss by going too fast—you also miss the sense of where you are going and why.

Eddie Cantor

242

Many persons have a wrong idea of what constitutes true happiness. It is not attained through self-gratification but through fidelity to a worthy purpose.

Helen Keller

243

I am a kind of paranoiac in reverse. I suspect people of plotting to make me happy.

J. D. Salinger

244

Money never made a man happy yet, nor will it. There is nothing in its nature to produce happiness. The more a man has, the more he wants. Instead of its filling a vacuum, it makes one.

Ben Franklin

245 **The search for happiness is one of the chief sources of unhappiness.**

Eric Hoffer

246 Annual income twenty pounds, annual expenditure nineteen nineteen and six, result happiness. Annual income twenty pounds, annual expenditure twenty pounds ought and six, result misery.

Charles Dickens

247

So of cheerfulness, or a good temper—the more it is spent, the more of it remains.

Ralph Waldo Emerson

248

There is no stronger craving in the world than that of the rich for titles, except that of the titled for riches.

Hesketh Pearson

249

You cannot always have happiness, but you can always give happiness.

Author Unknown

250

Ask yourself whether you are happy, and you cease to be so.

John Stuart Mill

251

Grief can take care of itself, but to get the full value from joy you must have somebody to divide it with.

Mark Twain

252

One is never as unhappy as one thinks, nor as happy as one had hoped to be.

Francois Duc de La Rochefoucauld

253

He who has so little knowledge of human nature as to seek happiness by changing anything but his own disposition will waste his life away in fruitless efforts.

Samuel Johnson

254

If we'd stop trying to be happy we could have a pretty good time.

Edith Wharton

255 *Laughter is the shortest distance between two people.*

Victor Borge

INDIFFERENCE

256 Science may have found a
cure for most evils; but it has
found no remedy for the worst
of them all—the apathy of
human beings.

Helen Keller

257

The worst sin towards our fellow creatures is not to
hate them, but to be indifferent to them; that's the
essence of inhumanity.

George Bernard Shaw

258

Apathy is the glove into which evil slips its hand.

Bodie Thoene

259

"Would you tell me, please, which way I ought to go from here?" "That depends a good deal on where you want to get to," said the Cheshire Cat. "I don't much care where—" said Alice. "Then it doesn't matter which way you go," said the cat.

Lewis Carroll

260

The opposite of love is not hate, it's indifference. The opposite of art is not ugliness, it's indifference. The opposite of life is not death, it's indifference.

Elie Wiesel

JUST DO IT

261

Doing more things faster is no substitute for doing the right things.

Stephen R. Covey

262

The most decisive actions of our life—I mean those that are most likely to decide the whole course of our future—are, more often than not, unconsidered.

André Gide

263

If a thing is worth doing, it is worth doing badly.

G. K. Chesterton

264

Nothing will ever be attempted if all possible objections must be first overcome.

Samuel Johnson

265

Delay is preferable to error.

Thomas Jefferson

266

When all is said and done, a lot more is said than done.

Unattributed

267

Words without actions are the assassins of idealism.

Herbert Hoover

268

Opportunities are usually disguised as hard work, so most people don't recognize them.

Ann Landers

269

Some of the world's greatest feats were accomplished by people not smart enough to know they were impossible.

Unattributed

270

Use what talents you possess; The woods would be very silent if no birds sang there except those that sang best.

Henry Van Dyke

271

You miss 100 percent of the shots you never take.

Wayne Gretzky

272

The man who makes no mistakes does not usually make anything.

William Connor Magee

273

The difficult can be done immediately, the impossible takes a little longer.

Army Corp of Engineers

274

If you wait to do everything until you're sure it's right, you'll probably never do much of anything.

Win Borden

275

If the only tool you have is a hammer, you tend to see every problem as a nail.

Abraham Maslow

276

It is never too late to be what you might have been.

George Eliot

277

To have begun is to have done half the task; dare to be wise.

Horace

278

A journey of a thousand miles must begin with a single step. Hitch your wagon to a star.

Ralph Waldo Emerson

279

Only those who will risk going too far can possibly find out how far one can go.

T. S. Eliot

280

You must do the thing you think you cannot do.

Eleanor Roosevelt

281

To avoid criticism, do nothing, say nothing, be nothing.

Elbert Hubbard

282

Some people see things as they are and say why.
I dream things that never were and say "why not?"

George Bernard Shaw

283

I haven't failed; I've just found 10,000 ways that won't work.

Thomas Edison

284

Nothing can stop the man with the right mental attitude from achieving his goal; nothing on earth can help the man with the wrong mental attitude.

Thomas Jefferson

285

He that leaveth nothing to chance will do few things ill, but he will do very few things.

Lord Halifax

286

Being too careful is being too careless in a different direction.

Shraga Silverstein

287

The fundamental cause of trouble in the world today is that the stupid are cocksure while the intelligent are full of doubt.

Bertrand Russell

288

They always say time changes things, but you actually have to change them yourself.

Andy Warhol

289

We have too many high sounding words, and too few actions that correspond with them.

Abigail Adams

290

Actions lie louder than words.

Carolyn Wells

291

I have long since come to believe that people never mean half of what they say, and that it is best to disregard their talk and judge only their actions.

Dorothy Day

292 *Action is character.*

F. Scott Fitzgerald

KNOWLEDGE

293

All men by nature desire knowledge.

Aristotle

294

If a man empties his purse into his head, no one can take it away from him. An investment in knowledge always pays the best interest.

Benjamin Franklin

295

When you know a thing, to hold that you know it; and when you do not know a thing, to allow that you do not know it—this is knowledge.

Confucius

296

None of us is as smart as all of us.

Eric Schmidt

297

Information is power.

Eric Schmidt

298

The beginning of knowledge is the discovery of something we do not understand.

Frank Herbert

299

If knowledge can create problems, it is not through ignorance that we can solve them.

Isaac Asimov

300

If you have knowledge, let others light their candles at it.

Margaret Fuller

301

To be absolutely certain about something, one must know everything or nothing about it.

Olin Miller

LIFE

302 Live your life in the manner that you would like your kids to live theirs.

Michael Levine

303 I recommend you to take care of the minutes, for hours will take care of themselves.

Lord Chesterfield

304

Dost thou love life? Then do not squander time; for that's the stuff life is made of.

Ben Franklin

305

The first step to getting the things you want out of life is this: Decide what you want.

Ben Stein

306

Life is full of surprises and serendipity. Being open to unexpected turns in the road is an important part of success. If you try to plan every step, you may miss those wonderful twists and turns. Just find your next adventure—do it well, enjoy it—and then, not now, think about what comes next.

Condoleezza Rice

307

Life is something that everyone should try at least once.

Henry J. Tillman

308

Life is what happens to you while you're busy making other plans.

John Lennon

309

Many peoples' tombstones should read "Died at 30, buried at 60."

Nicholas Murray Butler

310

Millions long for immortality who don't know what to do with themselves on a rainy Sunday afternoon.

Susan Ertz

311

Life is now in session.
Are you present?

B. Copeland

312

Life is like a ten-speed bicycle.
Most of us have gears we never use.

Charles M. Schulz

313

Most people believe they see the world as it is.
However, we really see the world as we are.

Unattributed

314

We are always beginning to live,
but are never living.

Marcus Manilius

315

Life is a foreign language: all men mispronounce it.

Christopher Morley

316

We teach everything but how to live. We have even forgotten that it is a subject.

Shraga Silverstein

317

May you live all the days of your life.

Jonathan Swift

318

We are always getting ready to live, but never living.

R. W. Emerson

319

How we spend our days is,
of course, how we spend
our lives.

Annie Dillard

320

Life is the art of drawing without an eraser.

John Gardner

321

Get busy living, or get busy dying.

Stephen King

MONEY

322

The problem with borrowing money is that as soon as one has, one inevitably begins to think of it as one's own. One becomes used to it, treats it like family, and may even come to resent or lose sight of the fact that it must all someday leave to visit someone else.

Andrew Tobias

323

There was a time when a fool and his money were soon parted, but now it happens to everybody.

Adlai E. Stevenson .

324

He is not fit for riches who is afraid to use them.

Thomas Fuller

325

Wealth is not without its disadvantages, and the case to the contrary, although it has often been made, has never proved widely persuasive.

Unattributed

326

Money is like muck, not good except it be spread.

Francis Bacon

327

The man is the richest whose pleasures are the cheapest.

Henry David Thoreau

328

There is some magic in wealth, which can thus make persons pay their court to it, when it does not even benefit themselves. How strange it is that a fool or knave, with riches, should be treated with more respect by the world than a good man or a wise man in poverty!

Ann Radcliffe

329

He that is of the opinion money will do everything may well be suspected of doing everything for money.

Benjamin Franklin

330

If you would be wealthy, think of saving as well as getting.

Benjamin Franklin

331

Riches may enable us to confer favors, but to confer them with propriety and grace requires a something that riches cannot give.

Charles Caleb Colton

332

Endless money forms the sinews of war.

Cicero

333

I'm living so far beyond my income that we may almost be said to be living apart.

e e cummings

334

The mint makes it first, it is up to you to make it last.

Evan Esar

335

The world is progressing and resources are becoming more abundant. I'd rather go into a grocery store today than to a king's banquet a hundred years ago.

Bill Gates

336

A great fortune is a great slavery.

Seneca

337

Men do not desire merely to be rich, but to be richer than other men.

John Stuart Mill

MORALITY, GOOD, AND EVIL

338

The world is well supplied with rude people spouting high moral positions about human rights, but it is noticeably lacking in those who worry about the human being waiting in line behind them at the automated-teller machine while they balance their checkbooks.

Owen Edwards

339

It is better to be hated for what you are than to be loved for something you are not.

Andre Gide

340

An ethical person ought to do more than he's required to do and less than he's allowed to do.

Michael Josephson

341

It is often easier to fight for principles than to live up to them.

Adlai E. Stevenson

342

The only thing necessary for the triumph of evil is for good men to do nothing.

Edmund Burke

343

Aim above morality. Be not simply good; be good for something.

Henry David Thoreau

344

The higher the buildings, the lower the morals.

Noel Coward

345

I have never believed there was one code of morality for a public and another for a private man.

Thomas Jefferson

NATURE

346

I speak for the trees, for the trees have no tongues.

Dr. Seuss

347

Unless someone like you cares a whole awful lot, nothing is going to get better. It's not.

Dr. Seuss

348

The refreshing pleasure from the first view of nature, after the pain of illness, and the confinement of a sick-chamber, is above the conceptions, as well as the descriptions, of those in health.

Ann Radcliffe

349

What is the use of a house if you haven't got a tolerable planet to put it on?

Henry David Thoreau

350

We shall never understand the natural environment until we see it as a living organism. Land can be healthy or sick, fertile or barren, rich or poor, lovingly nurtured or bled white. Our present attitudes and laws governing the ownership and use of land represent an abuse of the concept of private property…Today you can murder land for private profit. You can leave the corpse for all to see and nobody calls the cops.

Paul Brooks

351

Mountains inspire awe in any human person who has a soul. They remind us of our frailty, our unimportance, of the briefness of our span upon this earth. They touch the heavens, and sail serenely at an altitude beyond even the imaginings of a mere mortal.

Elizabeth Aston

OPPORTUNITY

352

When written in Chinese the word crisis is composed of two characters. One represents danger and the other represents opportunity.

John F. Kennedy

353

Opportunity: Opportunity's favorite disguise is trouble.

Frank Tiger

354

The reward for work well done is the opportunity to do more.

Jonas Salk

355

Small opportunities are often the beginning of great enterprises.

Demosthenes

356

You have to recognize when the right place and the right time fuse and take advantage of that opportunity. There are plenty of opportunities out there. You can't sit back and wait.

Ellen Metcalf

357

Trouble is only opportunity in work clothes.

Henry J. Kaiser

358

No great man ever complains of want of opportunity.

Ralph Waldo Emerson

359

A wise man will make more opportunities than he finds.

Sir Francis Bacon

360

You create your opportunities
by asking for them.

Patty Hansen

361

Too many people are thinking of
security instead of opportunity.
They seem more afraid of life
than death.

James F. Byrnes

362 *If opportunity doesn't knock, build a door.*

Milton Berle

363

I was seldom able to see an opportunity until it had ceased to be one.

Mark Twain

PARENTING

364

Biologically, adults produce children. Spiritually, children produce adults. Most of us do not grow up until we have helped children do so. Thus do the generations form a braided cord.

George F. Will

365

Sooner or later we all quote our mothers.

Bern Williams

366

No matter how old a mother is, she watches her middle-aged children for signs of improvement.

Florida Scott Maxwell

367

Happiness is having a large, loving, caring, close-knit family in another city.

George Burns

368

If you ever start feeling like you have the goofiest, craziest, most dysfunctional family in the world, all you have to do is go to a state fair. Because five minutes at the fair, you'll be going, "you know, we're alright. We are dang near royalty."

Jeff Foxworthy

369

I think people that have a brother or sister don't realize how lucky they are. Sure, they fight a lot, but to know that there's always somebody there, somebody that's family.

Trey Parker and Matt Stone

370

I would be the most content if my children grew up to be the kind of people who think decorating consists mostly of building enough bookshelves.

Anna Quindlen

371

Human beings are the only creatures that allow their children to come back home.

Bill Cosby

372

People who get nostalgic about childhood were obviously never children.

Bill Watterson

373

If you can give your son or daughter only one gift, let it be enthusiasm.

Bruce Barton

374

If your parents never had children, chances are you won't either.

Dick Cavett

375

The best way to keep children home is to make the home atmosphere pleasant—and let the air out of the tires.

Dorothy Parker

376

That's the funny thing about havin' a kid. They come with their own set of problems; make everything else you were worried about seem kinda silly.

Greg Garcia

377

It is not giving children more that spoils them;
it is giving them more to avoid confrontation.

John Gray

378 *By the time a man realizes that maybe his father was right, he usually has a son who thinks he's wrong.*

Charles Wadsworth

379

The art of mothering is to teach the art of living to children.

Elaine Heffner

380

It does not always follow that good men are good fathers.

Kathryn L. Nelson

381

I am amused when goody-goodies proclaim, from the safety of their armchairs, that children are naturally prejudice-free, that they only learn to "hate" from listening to bigoted adults. Nonsense. Tolerance is a learned trait, like riding a bike or playing the piano. Those of us who actually live among children, who see them in their natural environment, know the truth: Left to their own devices, children will gang up on and abuse anyone who is even slightly different from the norm.

Josh Lieb

382

People who say they sleep like a baby usually
don't have one.

Leo J. Burke

383

A mother who is really a mother
is never free.

Honore de Balzac

384

Each day of our lives we make
deposits in the memory banks
of our children.

Charles R. Swindoll

385

Every cliché about kids is true; they grow up so quickly,
you blink and they're gone, and you have to spend the
time with them now. But that's a joy.

Liam Neeson

386

Nothing you do for children is ever wasted. They seem not to notice us, hovering, averting our eyes, and they seldom offer thanks, but what we do for them is never wasted.

Garrison Keillor

387

You can learn many things from children. How much patience you have, for instance.

Franklin P. Jones

388

It is a sad commentary of our times when our young must seek advice and counsel from "Dear Abby" instead of going to Mom and Dad.

Abigail Van Buren (Dear Abby)

389
Fathers and mothers have lost the idea that the highest aspiration they might have for their children is for them to be wise…specialized competence and success are all that they can imagine.

Allan Bloom

390
A baby is born with a need to be loved—and never outgrows it.

Frank A. Clark

391

Always kiss your children goodnight, even if they're already asleep.

H. Jackson Brown, Jr.

392

The only way we can ever teach a child to say "I'm sorry" is for him to hear it from our lips first.

Kevin Leman

393

Even as kids reach adolescence, they need more than ever for us to watch over them. Adolescence is not about letting go. It's about hanging on during a very bumpy ride.

Ron Taffel

394

It's not only children who grow. Parents do too. As much as we watch to see what our children do with their lives, they are watching us to see what we do with ours. I can't tell my children to reach for the sun. All I can do is reach for it myself.

Joyce Maynard

395

Before I got married I had six theories about bringing up children; now I have six children and no theories.

John Wilmot

396 *Babies are always more trouble than you thought—and more wonderful.*

Charles Osgood

397

Parenting is not an intellectual endeavor. It does not emanate from the head. If it did, the smartest people would be the best parents, and I have never noticed that. Good parenting is rooted in a matter of how rooted you are in the steady soil of common sense. The heart and the gut are what make a good parent, not the head.

Charles Osgood

398

Children have never been very good at listening to their elders, but they have never failed to imitate them.

James Baldwin

399

Children need models more than they need critics.

Joseph Joubert

400

How sharper than a serpent's tooth it is to have a thankless child!

Shakespeare

401

If you bungle raising your children, I don't think whatever else you do well matters very much.

Jacqueline Kennedy Onassis

402

The commonest fallacy among women is that simply having children makes one a mother—which is as absurd as believing that having a piano makes one a musician.

Sydney J. Harris

403

When I was a boy of fourteen, my father was so ignorant I could hardly stand to have the old man around. But when I got to be twenty-one, I was astonished at how much he had learned in seven years.

Mark Twain

404

Babies help us to put the changing world into perspective too. Changing the world has to wait when it's time to change the baby.

Charles Osgood

QUOTATIONS

405

The wisdom of the wise and the experience of the ages is preserved into perpetuity by a nation's proverbs, fables, folk sayings, and quotations.

William Feather

406

A quotation in a speech, article, or book is like a rifle in the hands of an infantryman. It speaks with authority.

Brendan Francis

407

Quotes are nothing but inspiration for the uninspired.

Richard Kemph

408

I have suffered a great deal from writers who have quoted this or that sentence of mine either out of its context or in juxtaposition to some incongruous matter which quite distorted my meaning, or destroyed it altogether.

Alfred North Whitehead

409

Quotation, n: The act of repeating erroneously the words of another.

Ambrose Bierce

410

One must be a wise reader to quote wisely and well.

Amos Bronson Alcott

411

Write a wise saying and your name will live forever.

Anonymous

412

The wisdom of the wise, and the experience of ages, may be preserved by quotation.

Benjamin Disraeli

413

I never have found the perfect quote. At best I have been able to find a string of quotations which merely circle the ineffable idea I seek to express.

Caldwell O'Keefe

414

People will accept your ideas much more readily if you tell them Benjamin Franklin said it first.

David H. Comins

415

What's the use of a good quotation if you can't change it?

Doctor Who

416

A facility for quotation covers the absence of original thought.

Dorothy L. Sayers

417

A fine quotation is a diamond on the finger of a man of wit, and a pebble in the hand of a fool.

Joseph Roux

418

What a good thing Adam had. When he said a good thing he knew nobody had said it before.

Mark Twain

RESPONSIBILITY

419

You cannot escape the responsibility of tomorrow by evading it today.

Abraham Lincoln

420

To give up the task of reforming society is to give up one's responsibility as a free man.

Alan Paton

421

I think of a hero as someone who understands the degree of responsibility that comes with his freedom.

Bob Dylan

422

The perfect bureaucrat everywhere is the man who manages to make no decisions and escape all responsibility.

Brooks Atkinson

423

Action springs not from thought, but from a readiness for responsibility.

G. M. Trevelyan

424

Liberty means responsibility.
That is why most men dread it.

George Bernard Shaw

425

Character—the willingness to accept responsibility
for one's own life—is the source from which self-
respect springs.

Joan Didion

426

I believe that every right
implies a responsibility; every
opportunity, an obligation;
every possession, a duty.

John D. Rockefeller Jr.

427

The price of greatness
is responsibility.

Sir Winston Churchill

428

There is an expiry date on blaming your parents for steering you in the wrong direction. The moment you are old enough to take the wheel, the responsibility lies with you.

J. K. Rowling

SUCCESS

429

If A equals success, then the formula is: A = X + Y + Z, X is work. Y is play. Z is keep your mouth shut.

Albert Einstein

430

Along with success comes a reputation for wisdom.

Euripides

431

If your success is not on your own terms, if it looks good to the world but does not feel good in your heart, it is not success at all.

Anna Quindlen

432

I've come to embrace the notion that I haven't done enough in my life. I've come to confirm that one's title, even a title like President of the United States, says very little about how well one's life has been led. No matter how much you've done or how successful you've been, there's always more to do, always more to learn, and always more to achieve.

Barack Obama

433

I don't know the key to success, but the key to failure is trying to please everybody.

Bill Cosby

434 Success in business requires training and discipline and hard work. But if you're not frightened by these things, the opportunities are just as great today as they ever were.

David Rockefeller

435 Aim for success, not perfection. Never give up your right to be wrong, because then you will lose the ability to learn new things and move forward with your life.

David M. Burns

436

Success is the sum of small efforts repeated day in and day out.

Robert Collier

437

By working faithfully eight hours a day, you may eventually get to be a boss and work twelve hours a day.

Robert Frost

438

Success is going from failure to failure without a loss of enthusiasm.

Winston Churchill

439

There is no elevator to success. You have to take the stairs.

Unattributed

440

Try not to become a man of success but rather try to become a man of value.

Albert Einstein

441

The only place success comes before work is in the dictionary.

Vince Lombardi

442

There is the greatest practical benefit in making a few failures early in life.

Thomas Henry Huxley

443

No pessimist ever discovered the secrets of the stars or sailed to an uncharted land or opened a new heaven to the human spirit.

Helen Keller

444

You're never a loser until you quit trying.

Mike Dikta

445

We are all of us failures—at least, the best of us are.

J.M. Barrie

446

Nothing succeeds like success.

Alexandre Dumas

447

The first Clarke Law states, "If an elderly but distinguished scientist says that something is possible he is almost certainly right, but if he says that it is impossible he is very probably wrong."

Arthur C. Clarke

448

If at first you don't succeed, try, try again.

William Edward Hickson

449

Many of life's failures are people who did not realize how close they were to success when they gave up.

Thomas Alva Edison

450

Two men look through the same bars: One sees the mud, and one the stars.

Frederick Langbridge

451

Fame always brings loneliness. Success is as ice cold and lonely as the North Pole.

Vicki Baum

452

It takes as much courage to have tried and failed as it does to have tried and succeeded.

Ann Morrow Lindbergh

453

No winter lasts forever; no spring skips its turn.

Hal Borland

454

The past should be a springboard, not a hammock.

Ivern Ball

TRUTH
AND FALSEHOOD

455

An error is the more dangerous
in proportion to the degree of
truth which it contains.

Henri-Frederic Amiel

456 *Truth is
generally the
best vindication
against slander.*

Abraham Lincoln

457

Chase after truth and you'll free yourself, even though you never touch its coattails.

Clarence Darrow

458

The public will believe anything, so long as it is not founded on truth.

Edith Sitwell

459

The truth is more important than the facts.

Frank Lloyd Wright

460

All truths are easy to understand once they are discovered; the point is to discover them.

Galileo Galilei

461

A lie told often enough becomes the truth.

Lenin

462

A lie can travel halfway around the world while the truth is putting on its shoes.

Mark Twain

463

The history of our race, and each individual's experience, are sown thick with evidence that a truth is not hard to kill and that a lie told well is immortal.

Mark Twain

464

Truth sits upon the lips of dying men.

Matthew Arnold

465

How often have I said to you that when you have eliminated the impossible, whatever remains, however improbable, must be the truth?

Sir Arthur Conan Doyle

466

All truth passes through three stages. First, it is ridiculed. Second, it is violently opposed. Third, it is accepted as being self-evident.

Arthur Schopenhauer

467

It is one thing to show a man that he is in an error, and another to put him in possession of truth.

John Locke

468

Integrity is telling myself the truth. And honesty is telling the truth to other people.

Spencer Johnson

469

A lie has speed, but truth has endurance.

Unattributed

470

As scarce as truth is, the supply has always been in excess of demand.

Josh Billings

471

It takes two to speak the truth—one to speak and another to hear.

Henry David Thoreau

472

It is hard to believe that a man is telling the truth when you know that you would lie if you were in his place.

H. L. Mencken

473

Let us begin by committing ourselves to the truth—to see it like it is and tell it like it is—to find the truth, to speak the truth, and to live the truth.

Richard Nixon (1968)

474

Men occasionally stumble over the truth, but most of them pick themselves up and hurry off as if nothing had happened.

Sir Winston Churchill

475

Tell people the truth because they know the truth anyway.

Jack Welch

476

Being truthful, when you know it will cost you, is the true test of honesty.

Dave Weinbaum

477

The most dangerous of all falsehoods is a slightly distorted truth.

G. C. Lichtenberg

VIOLENCE, WAR, AND DISAGREEMENT

478

Those who make peaceful revolution impossible will make violent revolution inevitable.

John F. Kennedy

479

There are more pleasant things to do than beat up people.

Muhammad Ali

480

Nations have recently been led to borrow billions for war; no nation has ever borrowed largely for education. Probably,

no nation is rich enough to pay
for both war and civilization. We
must make our choice; we cannot
have both.

Abraham Flexner

481

I know not with what weapons World
War III will be fought, but World
War IV will be fought with sticks
and stones.

Albert Einstein

482

The quickest way of ending a war
is to lose it.

George Orwell

483

War is a series of catastrophes that results in a victory.

Georges Clemenceau

484

War is much too serious a matter to be entrusted to the military.

Georges Clemenceau

485

Neither enemy faces, nor the mothers that love them, come to mind when one is thinking of nothing but endeavoring to survive. Philosophizing about war is useless under fire.

Linda Berdoll

486

The only winner in the War of 1812 was Tchaikovsky.

Solomon Short

487

Wars are, of course, as a rule to be avoided; but they are far better than certain kinds of peace.

Theodore Roosevelt

488

War is a cowardly escape from the problems of peace.

Thomas Mann

489

War is an ugly thing, but not the ugliest of things. The decayed and degraded state of moral and patriotic feeling which thinks that nothing is worth war is much worse. The person who has nothing for which he is willing to fight, nothing which is more important than his own personal safety, is a miserable creature and has no chance of being free unless made and kept so by the exertions of better men than himself.

John Stuart Mill

490

Politics is war without bloodshed while war is politics with bloodshed.

Mao Tse-Tung

491

It is well that war is so terrible—otherwise we would grow too fond of it.

Robert E. Lee

492

Never, never, never believe any war will be smooth and easy, or that anyone who embarks on the strange voyage can measure the tides and hurricanes he will encounter. The statesman who yields to war fever must realize that once the signal is given, he is no longer the master of policy but the slave of unforeseeable and uncontrollable events.

Sir Winston Churchill

493

Appeasers believe that if you keep on throwing steaks to a tiger, the tiger will turn vegetarian.

Heywood Broun

494

Violence is the last refuge of the incompetent.

Isaac Asimov

495

You have not converted a man because you have silenced him.

Lord Morley

496

The use of force alone is but temporary. It may subdue for a moment; but does not remove the necessity of subduing again: and a nation is not governed, which is perpetually to be conquered.

Edmund Burke

497

Always remember others may hate you but those who hate you don't win unless you hate them. And then you destroy yourself.

Richard Nixon

498

I will permit no man to narrow and degrade my soul by making me hate him.

Booker T. Washington

499

Am I not destroying my enemies when I make friends of them?

Abraham Lincoln

500

War is nothing more than the continuation of politics by other means.

Karl von Clausewitz

501

The belief in the possibility of a short decisive war appears to be one of the most ancient and dangerous of human illusions.

Robert Lynd

APPENDIX: BONUS QUOTES

Every gun that is fired, every warship launched, every rocket fired, signifies, in the final sense, a theft from those who hunger and are not fed, those who are cold and are not clothed. The world in arms is not spending money alone. It is spending the sweat of its laborers, the genius of its scientists, the hopes of its children.

Dwight Eisenhower

Expecting the world to treat you fairly because you are a good person is like expecting a bull not to attack you because you are a vegetarian.

Dennis Wholey

In peace the sons bury their fathers, but in war the fathers bury their sons.

Croesus

You can't say civilization doesn't advance…in every war they kill you in a new way.

Will Rogers

I have nothing to offer but blood, toil, tears and sweat.

Winston Churchill

…we shall not flag or fail. We shall go on to the end. We shall fight in France, we shall fight on the seas and oceans, we shall fight with growing confidence and growing strength in the air, we shall defend our Island, whatever the cost may be. We shall fight on the beaches, we shall fight on the landing grounds, we shall fight in the fields and in the streets, we shall fight in the hills; we shall never surrender.

Winston Churchill

How vain it is to sit down to write when you have not stood up to live.

H. D. Thoreau

Man's mind—"the great indoors."

Shraga Silverstein

Some books are to be tasted, others to be swallowed, and some few to be chewed and digested.

Francis Bacon

Le sens commun n'est pas si commun. [Common sense is not so common.]

Voltaire

It takes more wisdom to know when to break plans than it does to make them.

Shraga Silverstein

Experience is not what happens to a man; it is what a man does with what happens to him.

Aldous Huxley

The trouble with most of us is that we would rather be ruined by praise than saved by criticism.

Norman Vincent Peale

We learn from experience that men never learn from experience.

Bernard Shaw

I don't divide the world into the weak and the strong, or the successes and the failures, those who make it or those who don't. I divide the world into learners and non-learners.

Benjamin Barber

The fewer the facts, the stronger the opinion.

Arnold H. Glasow

Wisdom too often never comes, and so one ought not to reject it merely because it comes late.

Felix Frankfurter

The art of being wise is the art of knowing what to overlook.

William James

Nine-tenths of wisdom is being wise in time.

Theodore Roosevelt

Learn from the mistakes of others; you can never live long enough to make them all yourself.

John Luther

There is only one thing more painful than learning from experience and that is not learning from experience.

Archibald McLeish

The important thing is to not stop questioning.

Albert Einstein

Experience is the name everyone gives to their mistakes.

Oscar Wilde

An expert is a man who has made all the mistakes, which can be made in a very narrow field.

Niels Bohr

If you believe everything you read, you better not read.

Japanese proverb

Never mistake knowledge for wisdom. One helps you make a living; the other helps you make a life.

Sandra Carey

Some people will never learn anything; for this reason, because they understand everything too soon.

Alexander Pope

Experience is a good teacher, but her fees are very high.

W. R. Inge

Wise men learn more from fools than fools from the wise.

Unattributed

A learned fool is one who has read everything and simply remembered it.

Josh Billings

It is better to remain silent and be thought a fool than to open one's mouth and remove all doubt.

Abraham Lincoln